SPIDERS AROUND THE WORLD

All About American HOUSE SPIDERS

John Bankston

Mitchell Lane
PUBLISHERS
2001 SW 31st Avenue
Hallandale, FL 33009
www.mitchelllanepub.com

Little Mitchie

First Edition, 2025.

Author: John Bankston
Designer: Ed Morgan
Editor: Morgan Brody

Little Mitchie is an imprint of Mitchell Lane Publishers.

Title: All About American House Spiders
Description: Hallandale, FL : Mitchell Lane Publishers, [2025]

Series: Spiders Around the World: North America
Library bound ISBN: 978-1-68020-936-5
eBook ISBN: 978-1-68020-941-9
Paperback ISBN: 979-8-89260-163-4

Photo credits: cover, pp. 8-9, 13-17, 20-21 wikicommons; pp. 4-7 Shutterstock; pp. 10-11 L Church/flickr.com; pp. 18-19 freepik.com

Contents

The trapped fly sticks to the house spider's web. It can't escape. The spider shoots webbing over the fly. Then it bites. **Venom** turns the bug's guts into liquid. The house spider drinks.

House spiders eat four times a day. That's a lot of bugs! They are great insect killers. They love flies, mosquitos, cockroaches, and ants. They don't harm people.

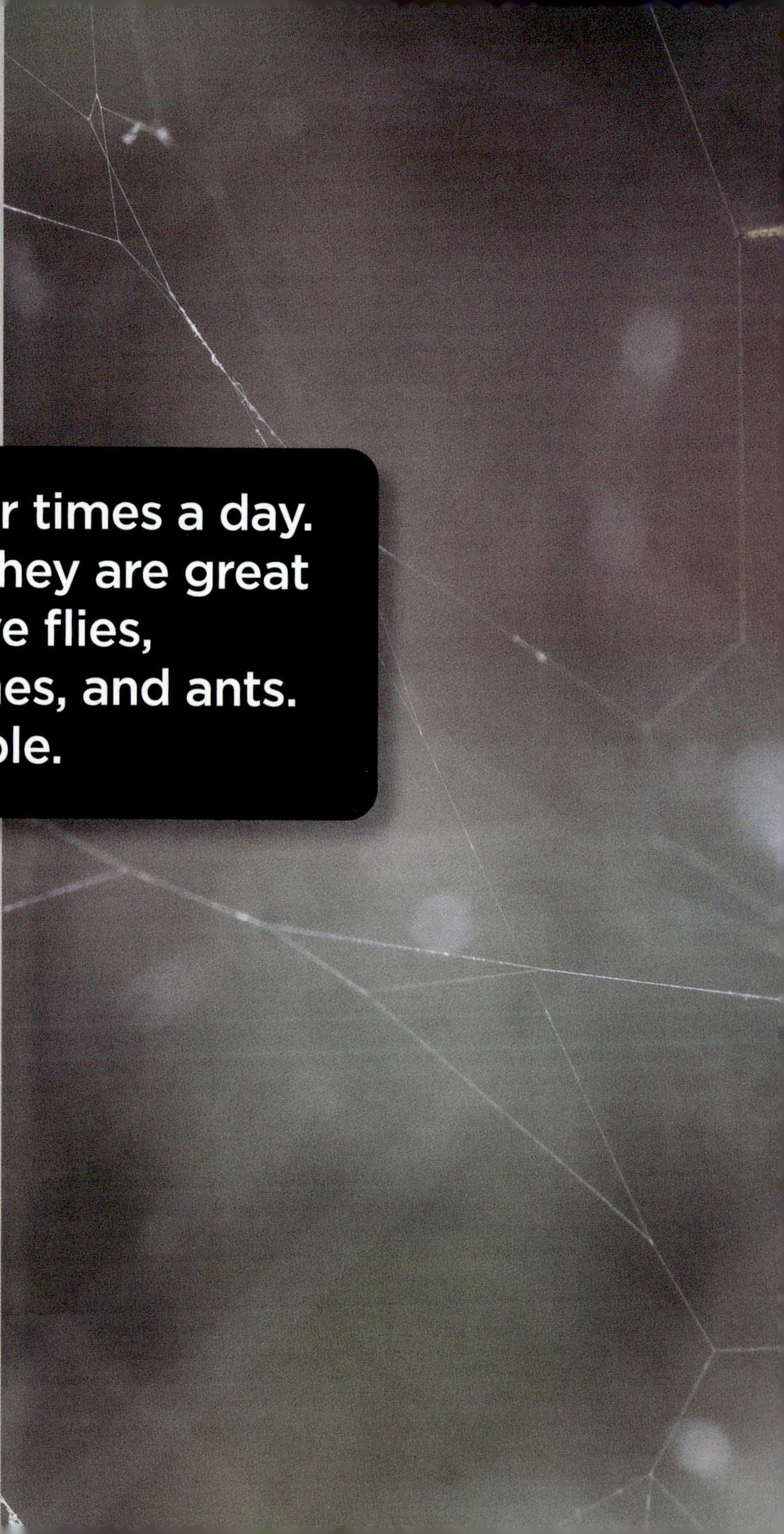

House spiders can be tan or dark brown or black. Males have orange and brown legs. They are just a quarter of an inch long. That's the size of a small button.

Female house spiders lay egg sacs. The light brown sacs hold 400 eggs. Females can produce 15 egg sacs a year. That's thousands of baby spiders (or spiderlings.)

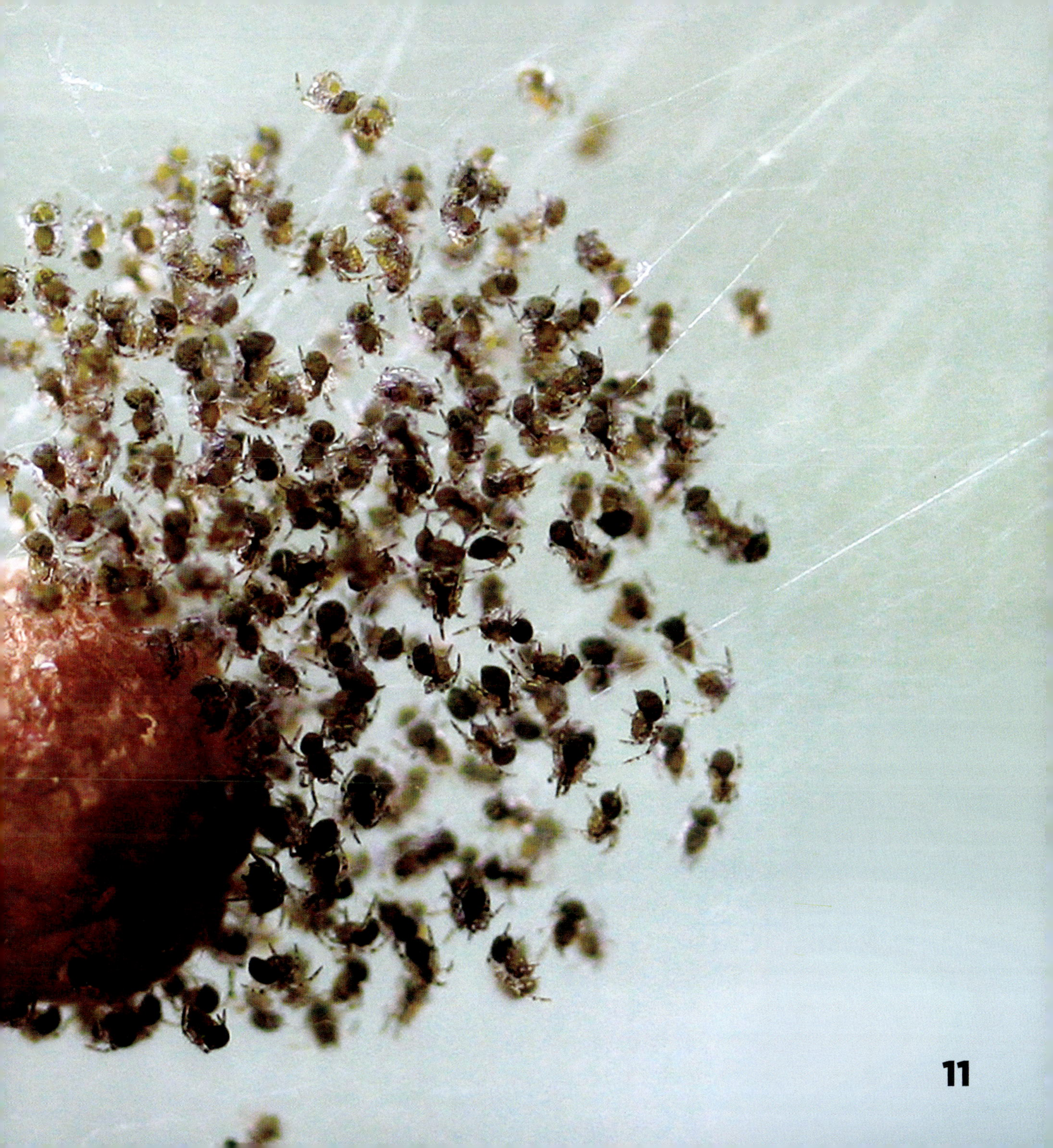

Females stick egg sacs to boxes. They hide them under chairs. If you move to another home, house spiders move with you.

Males roam. They run across your floor. The climb up walls. They are looking for food or female spiders.

House spiders aren't outdoor spiders. They like it warm. Moving one outside could kill it. North American wolf spiders look like house spiders. Their eyes cover their face. If you see one, you can move it outside.

House spiders don't just live in houses. They also live in sheds, barns, and garages. They are used to searching for water. They leave old webs everywhere. They are always making new ones. Most webs don't catch bugs.

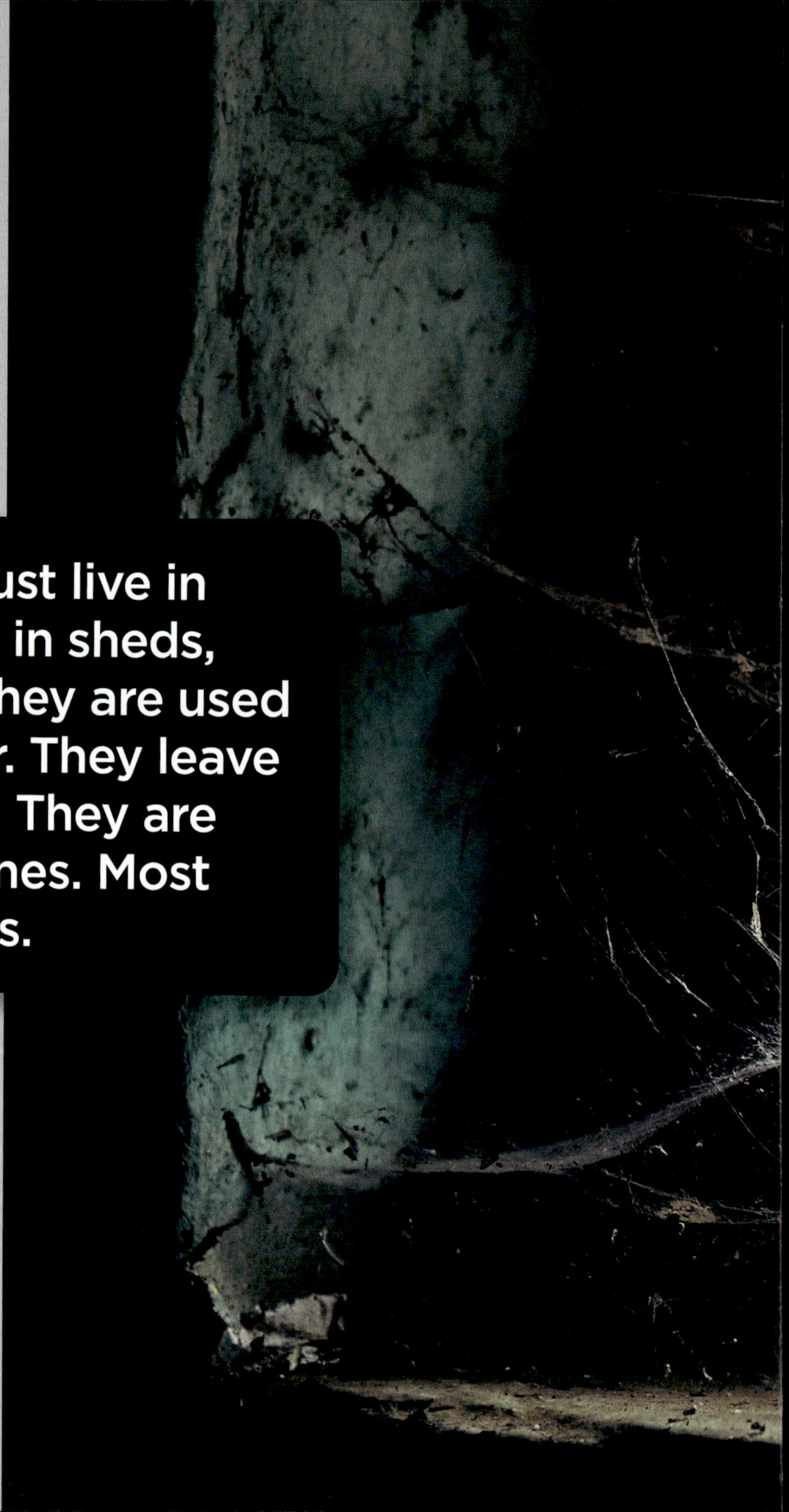

It's okay to sweep up old webs. Leave the ones they are living in. Your home can be insect-free thanks to a few house spiders.

Where Do **American House Spiders** Live?

The American house spider can be found across the United States. They also live in southern Canada.

Interesting Facts

- Spiders came before dinosaurs. House spiders have been living indoors for over two thousand years.
- American house spiders are **native** spiders. European house spiders came here in the 1600s.
- Male and female spiders often live on the same web.
- Spiders don't crawl out of drains. If you see one in a sink or tub, it climbed in looking for water.

Parts of an American House Spider

Spiders are not insects. They are **arachnids**. Their skeleton is outside of their body.

Abdomen
Because it is very rounded and much bigger than its head, it looks like a black widow spider. It doesn't have the widow's red hourglass.

Eyes
There are eight eyes on this spider. Four eyes on one side, four eyes on the other.

Legs
The legs can be twice as big as the body. House spiders have dark rings on their legs. The legs of a male look orange.

Glossary

abdomen **(ab-DOE-men)**
Place where the stomach is located

arachnids **(a-rack-NID)**
An eight-legged creature without antenna

native **(NAY-tuhv)**
Belonging to a person by birth or to a thing by nature

venom **(ven-OM)**
A dangerous liquid that is injected by an animal

Further Reading

All Things Spiders For Kids: Filled With Plenty of Facts, Photos, and Fun to Learn all About Spiders. Berlin, Germany: Admore Publishing, 2022.

Sovak, Jan. *Learning About Spiders*. Mineola, NY: Dover, 2019.

London, Martha. *Spiders*. Newburyport, MA: Focus Readers, 2020.

On the Internet

Discover some interesting facts about the House Spider on A-to-Z animals:
https://a-z-animals.com/animals/common-house-spider/

Learn more on DK Find Out:
https://www.dkfindout.com/uk/animals-and-nature/arachnids/house-spiders/#:~:text=

The National Wildlife Foundation has lots of helpful facts about house spiders:
https://www.nwf.org/Educational-Resources/Wildlife-Guide/Invertebrates/Common-House-Spider

Index